HONEYMAN'S
COLLECTION

5/-

THE

STRATHSPEY, REEL,

AND

HORNPIPE TUTOR.

BEING A CONCISE ANALYSIS OF THE PECULIAR METHOD OF BOWING THESE COMPOSITIONS, WITH NUMEROUS EXAMPLES, AND A SELECTION OF

92 FAVOURITE STRATHSPEYS AND REELS,

AND

50 FAVOURITE HORNPIPES,

WITH THE BOWING AND FINGERING MARKED THROUGHOUT EXACTLY AS THESE SHOULD BE PLAYED.

BY WM. C. HONEYMAN,

Author of "The Violin: How to Master It;" "The Secrets of Violin Playing;" "The Young Violinists Tutor and Duet Book;" "The Violin: How to Choose One;" "Scottish Violin Makers, Past and Present," &c., &c.

CONTENTS.

STRATHSPEYS, THEIR PECULIAR BOWING, ANALYSED AND EXPLAINED.

HORNPIPE PLAYING, THE DIFFERENT STYLES OF BOWING ANALYSED AND EXPLAINED.

EDINBURGH: E. KÖHLER & SON, 101 LEITH STREET.

LONDON: DUNCAN & CO., 186 FLEET STREET, FOULSHAM & CO., 4 PILGRIM STREET, LUDGATE HILL.

PRICE TWO SHILLINGS.

SCOTTISH STRATHSPEYS:

THEIR PECULIAR BOWING ANALYSED AND EXPLAINED.

[illegible]

Strathspey, Reel, and Hornpipe Tutor.

[illegible]

THE OBJECTS OF THIS WORK

[illegible]

SCOTTISH DANCE MUSIC.

[illegible]

Example No. 1.

[illegible]

Example No. 2.

[illegible]

bowing has more. The secret of the peculiar lameness I have alluded to—and I can find no better word to describe the bowing—is, I believe, that formerly this music was almost the only music of the ballroom. In those days there was a great deal of spirit in the dancing—including whisky—and little money was given to the poor fiddlers who were often kept toiling away at this heavy music for twelve hours at a stretch. Little wonder, then, that they discovered the easiest ways of producing the desired effect, and, having found them, adhered to them most religiously—laying down as a law to all who followed, that that and no other was *the style* in which the music must be played. An awkward crossing from one string to that above or below gave them no concern—to play both notes clean and distinct would have given them an amount of labour which their wearied and paralysed fingers would surely have refused to execute; they therefore solved the difficulty by neatly sounding both strings together, and gravely nodding on to the next passage. (See Example No. 7, second line). In like manner they found that all notes driven, like the first note in the second bar of "Doudle" strathspey, Example No. 5, could, with but a slight sacrifice of the rhythm, and no loss to the sharpness, be caught at the tip of the bow with a slight jerk of the wrist, off the preceding or leading note, instead of giving it a down bow to itself, and they adopted the plan without hesitation. This catching of the driven note is one of the most striking peculiarities of the Scottish strathspey. I never yet saw it explained in print; nay, I have met dozens of strathspey players who could do it, but who could not tell how it was done, and so were absolutely unable to impart the secret to another. Only the other day, when I had a visit from one of the best strathspey players in Scotland, I pointed out to him that he began "Tullochgorum" strathspey with a strongly accented down bow to the leading note before the bar, and showed him that the object was to catch the driven note at the beginning of the next bar off the tip of the bow with a jerk of the wrist, when he exclaimed in surprise, "Why, I have been playing strathspeys before the public for forty years, and yet I never understood that before, though I have been doing it all the time!"

No. 3.—The Notes and Bowing.

down up

If it is difficult to explain this trick of style orally, and with the violin in your hand, it is still more so to do it in print; but I shall here attempt the task, convinced that in so doing I will be benefiting many a puzzled learner, and so certain that, though I may not make the thing clear to all, I am giving the real solution of the mystery.

In the following example, which forms the opening bars of "Lasses look before you," the student has an easy and intelligible phrase; he

No. 4.

has dotted notes, played in the usual manner, that is, with one bow to each two notes, the short note being caught off the first with a slight jerk of the wrist, just as a crotchet and quaver are played in an Irish jig. So far all is plain sailing, as this kind of bowing is given in every exercise book, and is used in jigs, marches, strathspeys, and many other kinds of music. Even the down bow given in the next example need not

No. 5.

down up

puzzle the student much, as it is easy to push on the bow till the three notes are played, and then make up for the loss of bow by drawing the hair more quickly over the next two to get back to the upper part of the bow. It is, as I have already noticed, the *driven* notes which puzzle most; and to put their peculiarity of bowing lucidly before the student's eye—and through that impress it on his mind—I have designed the example.

No. 6.—"STUMPIE" (Strathspey, 2nd Part).

Written thus.

Played thus.

down up

The actual effect would be.

In the first line is given a phrase from "Stumpie" strathspey as it is usually written or printed. The novice, seeing the notes for the first time, would apply the ordinary rules of bowing to the passage, and give the first note, D, an up bow, and the second, or driven note, a down bow, and the third, the open string E, an up bow. But mark what would be the result. The next two notes, dotted in the ordinary manner, would get one down bow to the two; and then would come an insuperable obstacle—the playing of a driven note with an up bow. Indeed, the ordinary rules of bowing could not be continued through many bars of any strathspey without hopelessly enmeshing the student in difficulties. Let him now turn to the second line, and study closely the bowing as there marked. Although there is a slur over the first bar connecting the first two notes, it must not be thought that this implies the smoothness which a slur usually represents. At the end of the slur is a dot to show that the note is to be picked off sharply with a jerk of the wrist when the bow has passed across the string to near its point. The moment this note is sounded the bow is reversed for the open string note E, moving the hair rather more quickly across the string, so that a long sweep may be left for the next down bow, which has three notes linked on to it. The next note with the dot over it, D, is caught at the top of the bow with the same peculiar jerk of the wrist, which is really only another form of that used in Example No. 1, and so the time proceeds. Now, I have shown that our forerunners in violin playing, in hitting upon this bowing, as peculiar and easy of execution as it is inspiriting in its effect, actually discovered the only mode by which the music could be performed without landing the player in worse difficulties than those thus ingeniously surmounted. But the peculiar method—which has now become so inseparably wedded to the music as to be considered one of its constituent parts—was not a complete gain. If the student will get a good strathspey player to rattle through the second part of "Stumpie"—which he will do by bowing it exactly as I have marked it—and will listen attentively, he will find that there is a palpable sacrifice of the rhythm of the melody. What that effect is I have tried to visibly represent in the third line; but I may say that the representation there given would be nearer the real effect if the first bar were driven down through the middle of the second note G, and all the other bars in the line were jerked forward in like manner into the middle of the note behind which I have placed them. An attentive examination of the example will possibly call forth the exclamation, "Surely there is something wrong in that way of bringing the note forward before the bar, or even on to it," but, as I said in starting, Scottish music is amenable to no rule whatever. That is, undoubtedly, the effect produced; but whether it is wrong or right depends upon the standpoint from which we regard it. It is part of the music, bone of its bone and flesh of its flesh, and just as we are forced to accept without question the consecutive fifths already noticed—for no other harmony is possible—so must we accept the peculiar effect of these driven notes. It is this trick of style which so staggers and appals foreign or even English violinists. They cannot give even the feeblest imitation of the effect, though possibly masters of the instrument in every other sense; and when their most strenuous efforts only induce a smile from the experienced listener, sometimes lose temper, and innocently insist that they are playing the music as it is written. The student who masters this bowing is a long distance

No. 7.

FREEDOM OF BOWING.

INTONATION.

SPIRIT AND EXPRESSION.

No. 8.

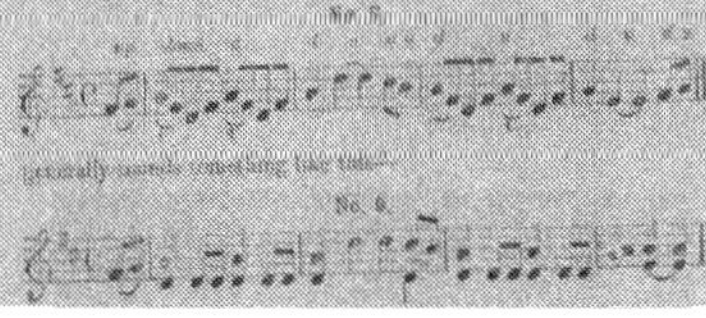

No. 9.

Friends of Wighton Shand Collection. Vol.15	Honeyman, William Crawford	Jimmy Shand Collection JS15. Honeyman's Collection [cover title]. *The Strathspey, Reel, and Hornpipe Tutor, being a concise analysis of the peculiar method of bowing these compositions, with numerous examples; and a selection of 92 favourite strathspeys and reels, and 50 favourite hornpipes ...* (Edinburgh & London: E. Kohler & Son, 1898)

REEL PLAYING.

In playing reels *only the upper half of the bow ought to be used*. A great deal of the spirit of a reel is given by accenting strongly the first and third beats of the bar, as in Example No. 10 ("Rachel Rae"); and

No. 10.

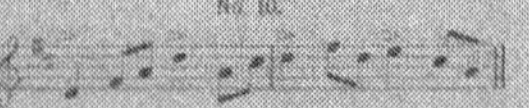

also by slurring and bowing alternately every two notes, as in Example No. 11 ("Fife Hunt"). An excellent exercise for this bowing will be

No. 11.

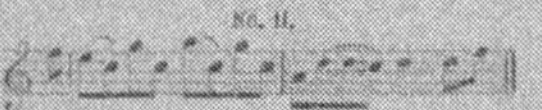

found on the upper half of page 43 of Leduc. Some reels, however, with much crossing of the strings, must have a bow to each note, as, for instance, the third complete bar in "The Deil among the Tailors." The reel should be practised rather slow at first, until every note can be sounded clear and smooth, when the proper speed can easily be given. Nearly all the studies in Kreutzer's famous book are marked moderato, which was doubtless a gentle hint on the part of the composer to the student to avoid scrambling through them. The same hint might reasonably be applied to the study of reel playing. They may be played ridiculously slow at first with the very best results, and even when mastered they should not be played at breakneck speed. There is a tendency among modern players to take reels too fast, and some have even begun to write them in semi-quavers, thus accentuating the mistake. In this book they are all written in the old style, in quavers, with the line drawn through the C at the beginning, which not only gives a clearer reading to the student, but may tend to keep him from that bane of all good violin playing, scrambling. "The more haste the less speed" applies to reel playing as well as to any other branch of violin playing. If you wish to have a clear and brilliant style, go slow at first—*moderato, moderato, moderato*.

THE MARKINGS.

Every up bow in the whole of this book is indicated by the sign ∨, and every down bow by the sign ⊓, which is preferable to using the letters *u* and *d*, as it makes the music intelligible to players of every nationality, and it is always better to use signs already in use than to introduce new ones. In both strathspeys and reels such phrases as—

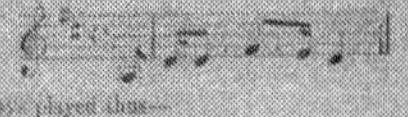

are nearly always played thus—

and the strathspeys and reels which follow are selected with a view to illustrating that bowing. In such phrases the first note with the down bow is cut very sharply, as if it were followed by a double dotted note instead of a single dotted one. The most difficult stroke of all, the driven note caught off another, is illustrated further on.

OPEN STRINGS

are to be used all through this work, except where the reverse is indicated by the figure 4. Much of the peculiar sharpness of the strathspey and reel depends upon the free use of open strings, as the fifths of a violin are of the full width, and not tempered as in the piano or organ. Double notes in unison are indicated by the figures $\frac{0}{4}$.

The following signs also are used:—

W.B.—Whole bow.
H.B.—Half bow.
P.—Point of the bow.
U.T.P.—Upper third part of the bow.
M.T.—Middle third part.
U.H.—Upper half.
⁀.—Two bows in the same direction.

THE EXPENDITURE OF THE BOW

in strathspey playing requires the most watchful and careful study on the part of the performer; indeed, many of the effects can be got at one part of the bow and at no other. The markings given throughout this work ought to enable the ordinary violin player to form an effective and correct style of expending the bow, which could be applied in playing at sight from any other collection of strathspeys, reels, or hornpipes not so rigidly marked.

LASSES, LOOK BEFORE YOU.

STRATHSPEY.

THE DUCHESS OF GORDON.

STRATHSPEY.

8
STIRLING CASTLE.
Strathspey.
THE FAIRY DANCE.
Reel.
THE BRIG O' DEE.
Strathspey.
D.C.

SOLDIERS' JOY.

Reel.

CLACHNACUDDIN.

Strathspey.

THE WIND THAT SHAKES THE BARLEY.

Reel.

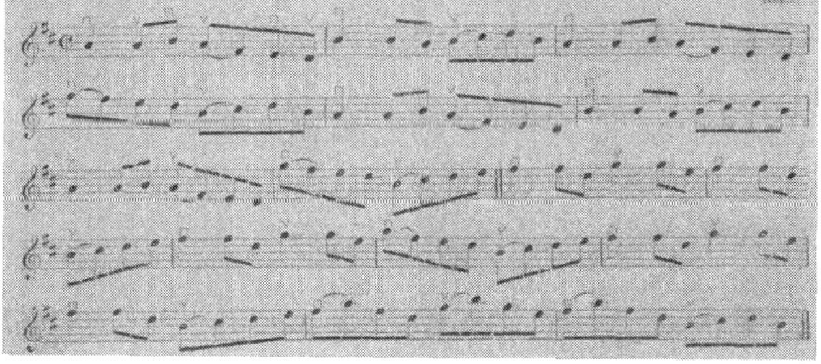

CAMERONS' GOT HIS WIFE AGAIN.

Strathspey.

THE LIMERICK LASSES.

Reel.

CARRICK'S RANT, OR THE SMITH'S A GALLANT FIREMAN.

Strathspey.

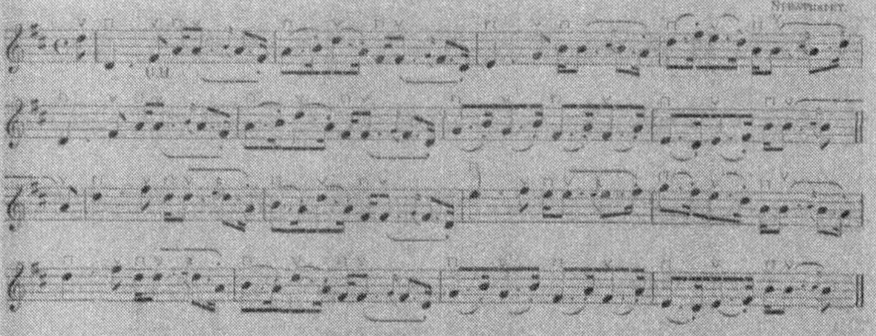

YE'RE WELCOME, CHARLIE STUART.

Reel.

DUNCAN DAVIDSON.

STRATHSPEY.

M.B.

THE BACK OF THE CHANGE HOUSE.

REEL.

THE MARQUIS OF HUNTLY.

STRATHSPEY.

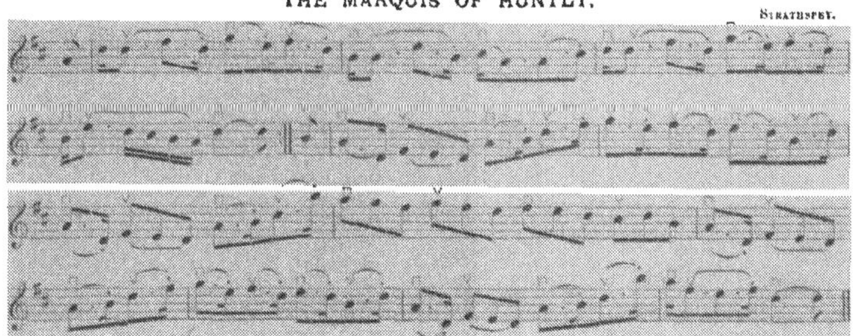

Friends of Wighton Shand Collection. Vol.15	Honeyman, William Crawford	Jimmy Shand Collection JS15, Honeyman's Collection [cover title]. *The Strathspey, Reel, and Hornpipe Tutor, being a concise analysis of the peculiar method of bowing these compositions, with numerous examples, and a selection of 92 favourite strathspeys and reels, and 50 favourite hornpipes ...* (Edinburgh & London: E. Kohler & Son, 1898)

12
TO MY BED I WINNA GANG.
Reel.
THE BRAES O' MAR.
Strathspey.
CLEAN PEA STRAE.
Reel.
LORD LYNDOCH.
Strathspey.

JENNY DANG THE WEAVER.

Reel.

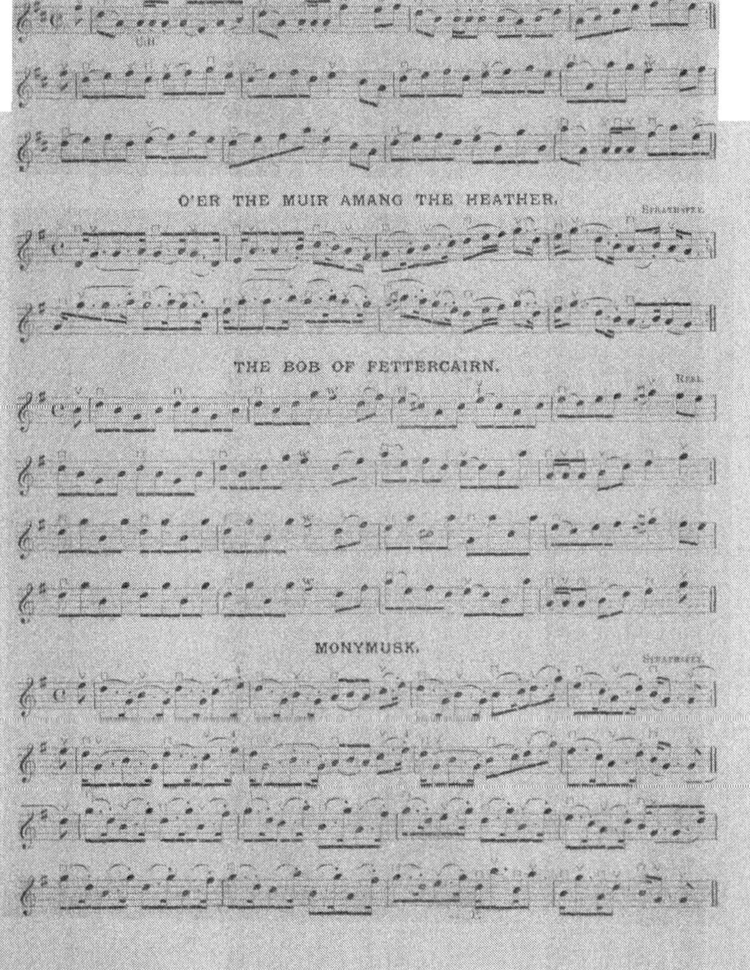

LORD MACDONALD.

PETER BAILIE.

SMALL COALS FOR NAILERS.

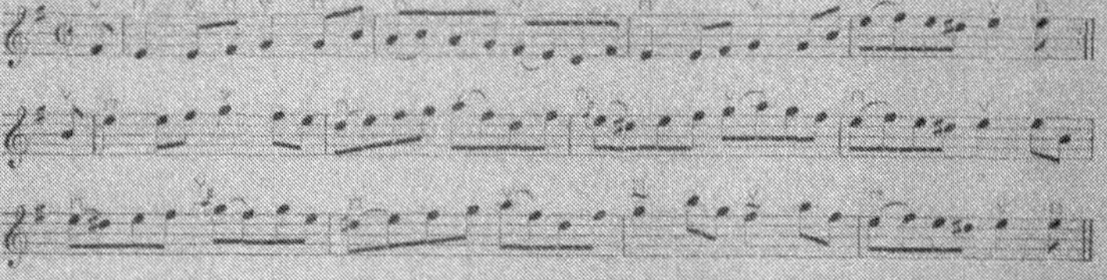

THE HAUGHS OF CROMDALE.

JOHNNY LAD.

Reel.

LADY LUCY RAMSAY.

Strathspey.

FIGHT ABOUT THE FIRESIDE.

Reel.

WELCOME TO YOUR FEET AGAIN.

Strathspey.

1st time. 2nd time.

CAPER FEY.
Reel.
CAWDOR FAIR.
Strathspey.
THE FIFE HUNT.
Reel.
GEORGE THE FOURTH.
Strathspey.
1st time.
2nd time.

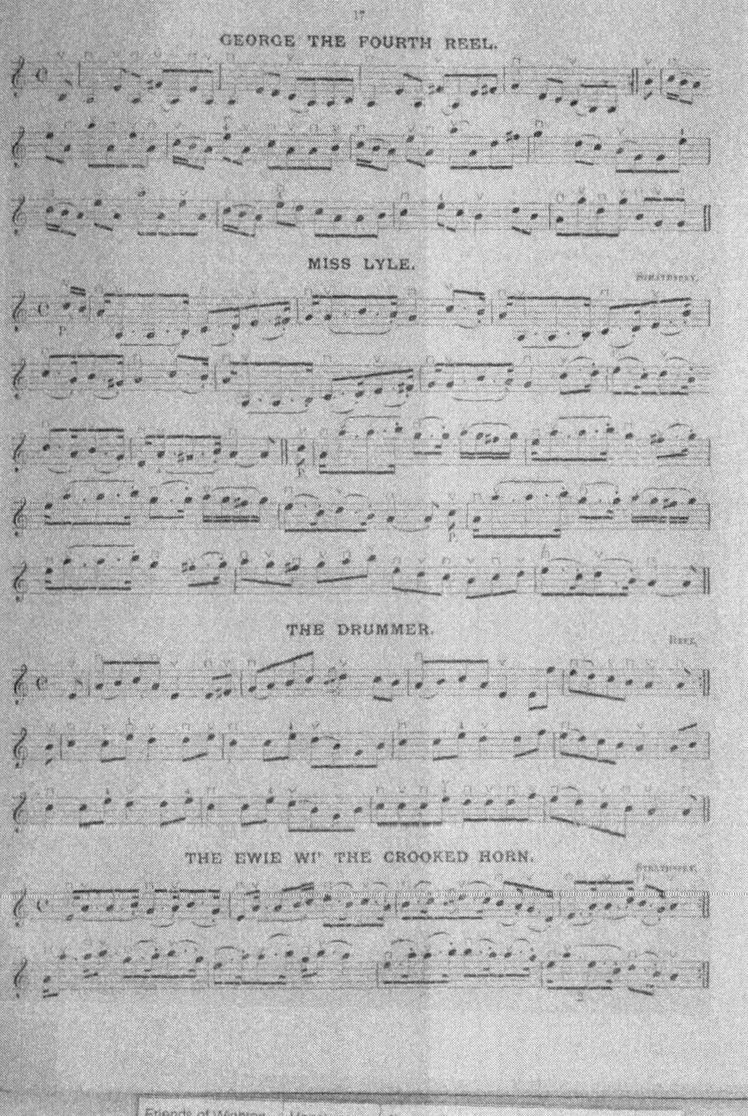
GEORGE THE FOURTH REEL.
MISS LYLE.
STRATHSPEY.
THE DRUMMER.
REEL.
THE EWIE WI' THE CROOKED HORN.
STRATHSPEY.

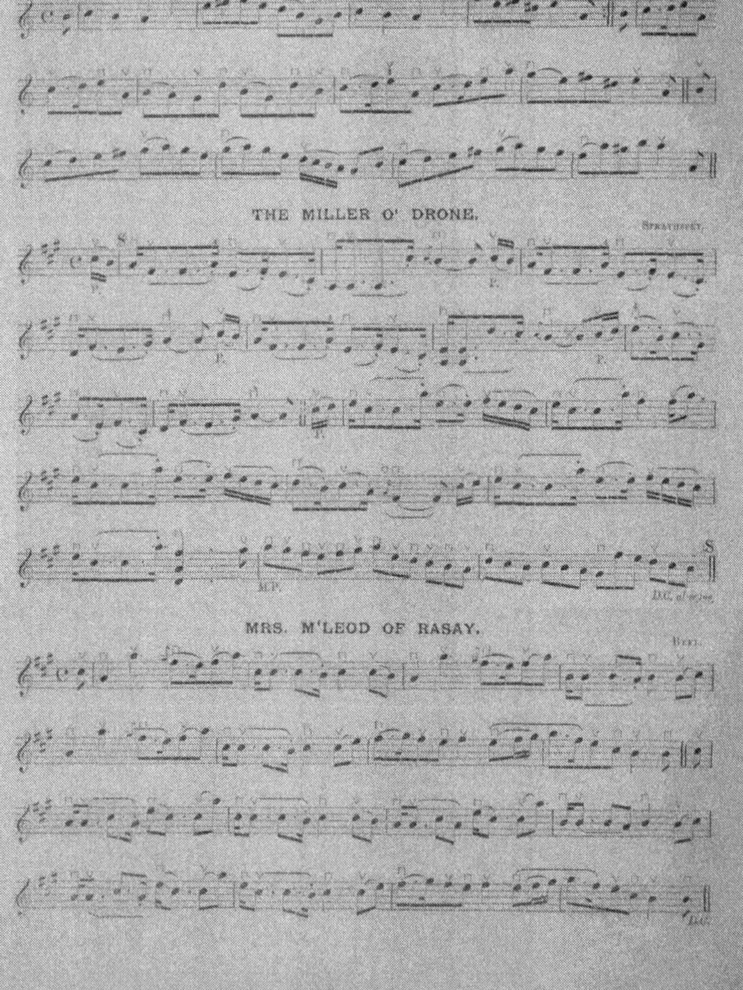
18
JENNY NETTLES.
Reel.
THE MILLER O' DRONE.
Strathspey.
D.C. al segno
MRS. M'LEOD OF RASAY.
Reel.
D.C.

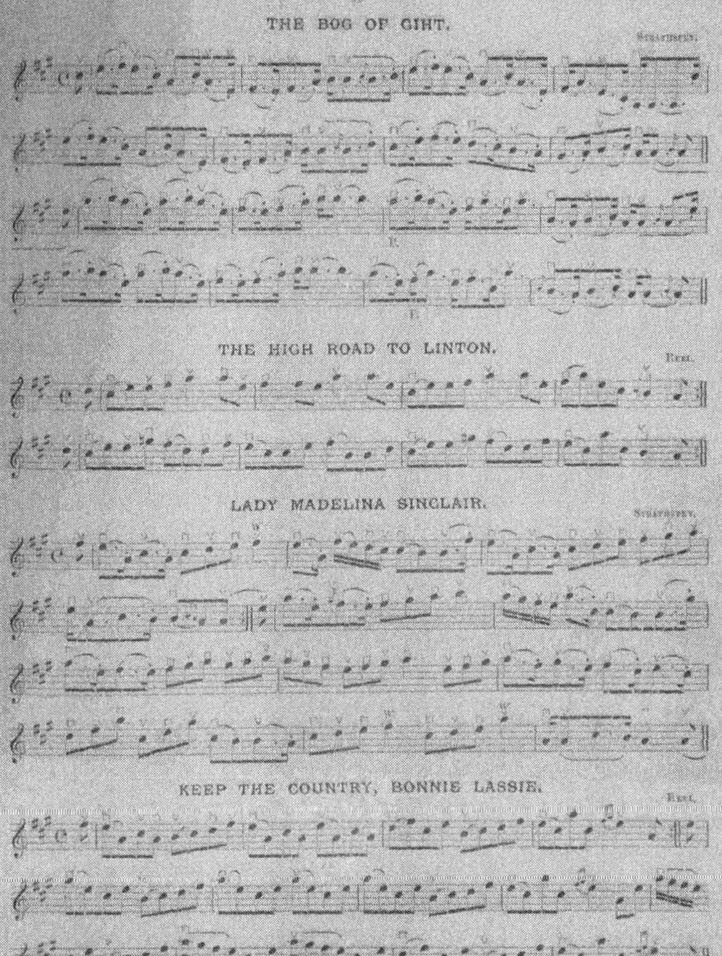
10
THE BOG OF GIHT.
STRATHSPEY.
THE HIGH ROAD TO LINTON.
REEL.
LADY MADELINA SINCLAIR.
STRATHSPEY.
KEEP THE COUNTRY, BONNIE LASSIE.
REEL.

GHILLIE CALLUM.

Strathspey for Sword Dance.

CUTTYMUN AND TREELADLE.

Reel.

THE BRIG O' PERTH.

Strathspey.

THE MARQUIS OF TULLYBARDINE.

Reel.

SOUTH OF THE GRAMPIANS.

Strathspey.

JENNY SUTTON.

Reel.

HIGHLAND WHISKY.

Strathspey.

W.B.

TIMOUR THE TARTAR.

Reel.

THE MARQUIS OF HUNTLY'S FAREWELL.

Strathspey.

TULLOCH, OR HUILICHAN.

Reel.

MISS DRUMMOND OF PERTH.

Strathspey.

MAJOR MOLE.

Reel.

DAINTY DAVIE.

Strathspey.

CLYDESIDE LASSES.

Reel.

D.C.

MRS. GARDEN OF TROUP.

Strathspey.

1st time. 2nd time.

LADY WALLACE.

Reel.

D.C.

JOHN ROY STEWART.

Strathspey.

MRS. CHARLES STEWART.

Reel

THE BRAES OF TULLYMET.

Strathspey

LADY SUTHERLAND.

Reel

Friends of Wighton Shand Collection. Vol.15	Honeyman, William Crawford	Jimmy Shand Collection JS15, Honeyman's Collection [cover title]. *The Strathspey, Reel, and Hornpipe Tutor, being a concise analysis of the peculiar method of bowing these compositions, with numerous examples, and a selection of 92 favourite strathspeys and reels, and 50 favourite hornpipes ...* (Edinburgh & London: E. Kohler & Son, 1898)

LORD RAMSAY.
STRATHSPEY.
THE ISLE OF SKYE.
REEL.
MASTER FRANCIS SITWELL.
STRATHSPEY.

MISS DUMBRECK.

Reel.

P.

BRECHIN CASTLE.

Strathspey.

LADY MONTGOMERY.

Reel.

P.

THE MARQUIS OF HUNTLY'S HIGHLAND FLING.

Strathspey.

Friends of Wighton Shand Collection, Vol.15	Honeyman, William Crawford	Jimmy Shand Collection JS15, Honeyman's Collection [cover title]. *The Strathspey, Reel, and Hornpipe Tutor, being a concise analysis of the peculiar method of bowing these compositions, with numerous examples, and a selection of 92 favourite strathspeys and reels, and 50 favourite hornpipes ...* (Edinburgh & London: E. Kohler & Son, 1898)

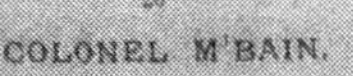

COLONEL M'BAIN.

Reel.

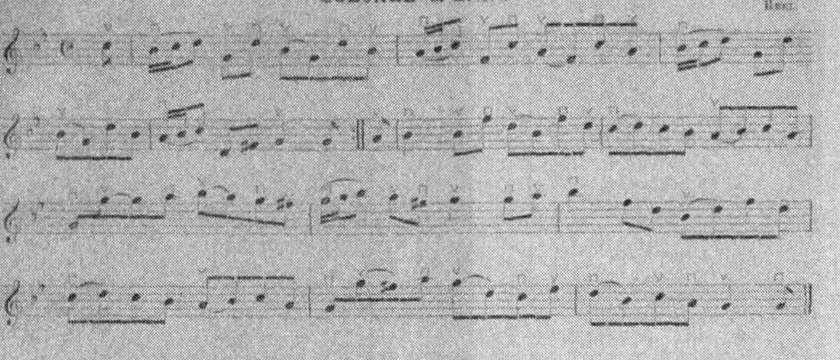

NEIL GOW'S SECOND WIFE.

Strathspey.

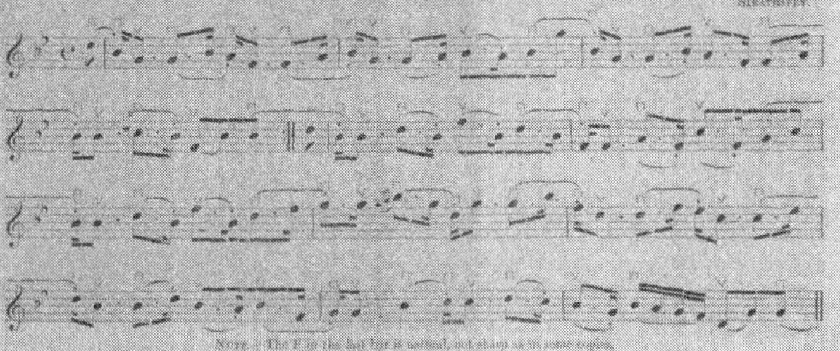

NOTE.—The F in the last bar is natural, not sharp as in some copies.

CAPTAIN KEELER.

Reel.

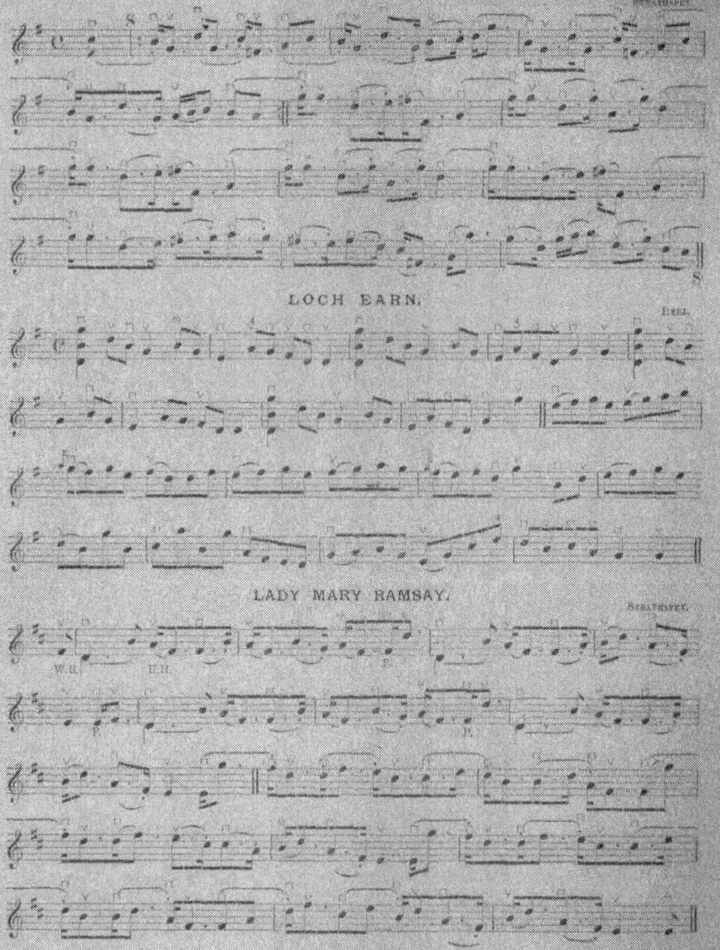
TULLOCHGORUM.
STRATHSPEY.
LOCH EARN.
REEL.
LADY MARY RAMSAY.
STRATHSPEY.
W.B.
H.H.

JENNY'S BAWBEE.

Reel.

NIEL GOW.

Strathspey.

W.B.

Moderato.

PERTHSHIRE HUNT.

Reel.

STUMPIE.

Strathspey.

WATERLOO.

Reel.

SLOW STRATHSPEYS.

THE DEAN BRIDGE OF EDINBURGH.

Slow Strathspey.

This lovely melody is given in some collections as a composition of Peter Milne's, but that is a mistake. It was written by the Rev. Mr. Tough, but improved by Peter Milne, who raised the first half of the second part an octave higher, though by doing so it is made to challenge comparison with the second part of "Lady Mary Ramsay," which Mr. Tough seems to have wished to avoid. It must be played with long sweeping bows, and makes a capital solo, followed with "Bank's Hornpipe" and finishing with the "Trumpet Hornpipe."

THE BRAES O' AUCHTERTYRE.

Slow Strathspey.

This grand melody was composed or adapted about the year 1723 by James Crachan, but was first transposed from the key of C to that of A, and played as a slow strathspey by James Scott Skinner.

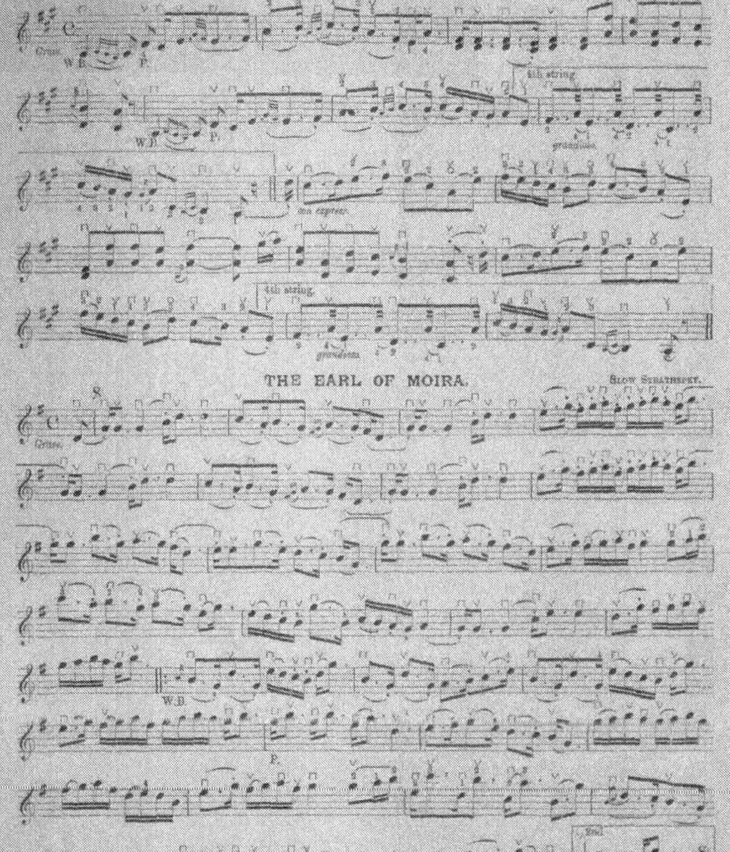

LORD JOHN CAMPBELL.

Slow Strathspey.

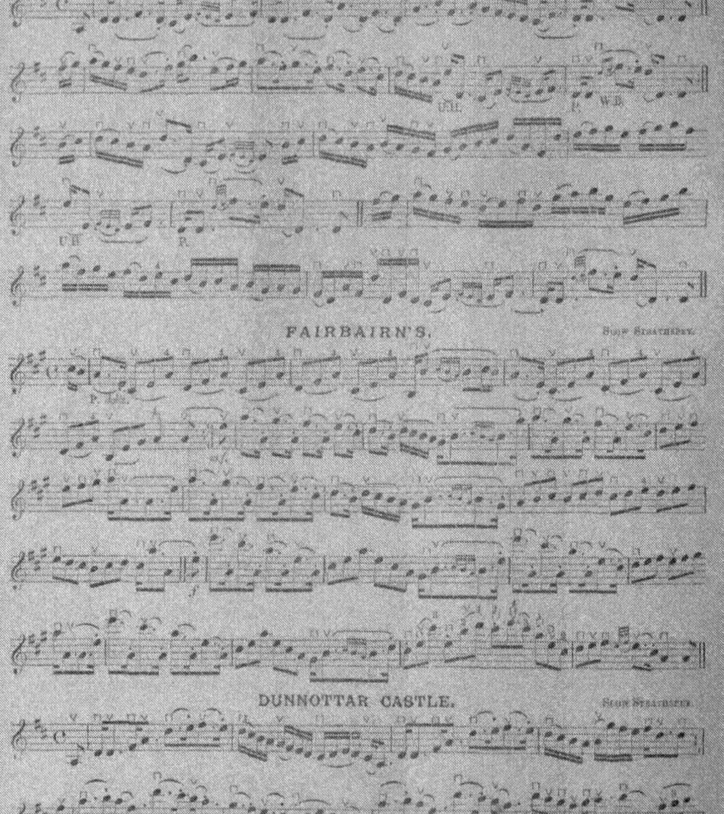

FAIRBAIRN'S.

Slow Strathspey.

DUNNOTTAR CASTLE.

Slow Strathspey.

HORNPIPE PLAYING:

THE DIFFERENT STYLES OF BOWING ANALYSED AND EXPLAINED.

There are three styles of bowing hornpipes. The first, which is almost identical with that of bowing reels, may be named "The Sailor's Hornpipe" style, and is shown further on in the "College Hornpipe." The second, which may be named the "Newcastle style," is used for clog dancing or other step dancing at an easier pace than "The Sailor's Hornpipe," and is shown in the following example, No. 12:—

No. 12.

This style, which is played mostly with the upper half of the bow, but permits a pretty free sweep of the stick, presents no great difficulty till the last note in the second last bar is reached. This note, E, is bowed with a *jerk* of the wrist, and not slurred over the bar like the others. When the student has mastered that trick, he will find the bowing of Example No. 13 not so stupendously difficult. In passing it may be noted that any student who can play Kreutzer's 28th Study can play both of these styles without an effort, but there are many excellent players, also, who never look at that study. The third style is rather more difficult of acquirement than the second, and may be named "The Sand Dance Style," as it produces a very sharp and distinct articulation of every note, and is very effective when played [illegible], as the music is generally wanted in a sand dance, in which every touch and slide of the foot on the sanded stage must be heard.—Example No. 13:—

No. 13.

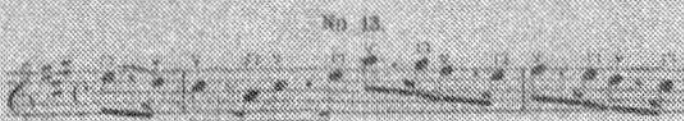

This peculiar stroke is sometimes called the "back bow," from the bow being moved back instead of forward. There are two kinds of "back bowing"—that in Example No. 13 being the most difficult. This bowing presents the peculiarity that it cannot be well played slow—that is, the effect is then all but lost to the ear—and the learner, of course, cannot at first play it fast. The other form of the "back bow" is that alluded to, and exemplified in Spohr's 21st and 31st Exercises, and is used in slow, quiet music for dotted notes which are not wished so sharp and crisp as those taught up in the usual way, two to each bow. This bowing of Spohr's, though it has never a graceful appearance to the eye, is often required when the bow needs righting, and also, as above noted, in particular kinds of music, such as *Adagios* and *Andantes*—and presents no great difficulty to the learner. It is the rapid form of the "back bow" which staggers most players. To master it the student must play with the upper *third part* of the bow only; playing the leading notes—namely, those immediately before the bar—with an inversion of the rules of bowing, that is, with a strongly accented down bow. The first note in the bar is then played with an up bow, the short note after it being then crisply caught with a quick down stroke. It must be played vigorously and with great spirit. No written description can convey any idea of the neat sprightliness of this style of bowing; and it is absolutely necessary that every violin player should master it, not for hornpipes alone, but for every kind of music which has groups of very quick dotted notes, such as, for instance, the second part of the "Massed Chorus," in *Naaman*, and dozens of other passages which will readily occur to the student.

Sometimes both the second and the third style may be effectively introduced in playing the same tune, while the first, or "Sailor's Hornpipe style," may come in very effectively when the pace is quickened towards the end of the dance, as it generally is for an effective exit, the speed, indeed, being generally supplied by orchestra more than the dancer, who is then nearly exhausted. I have, therefore, given several examples of the same tune written in the different styles.

THE WEST-END HORNPIPE.

An Easy Study in the Third Styles.

THE WEST-END HORNPIPE.

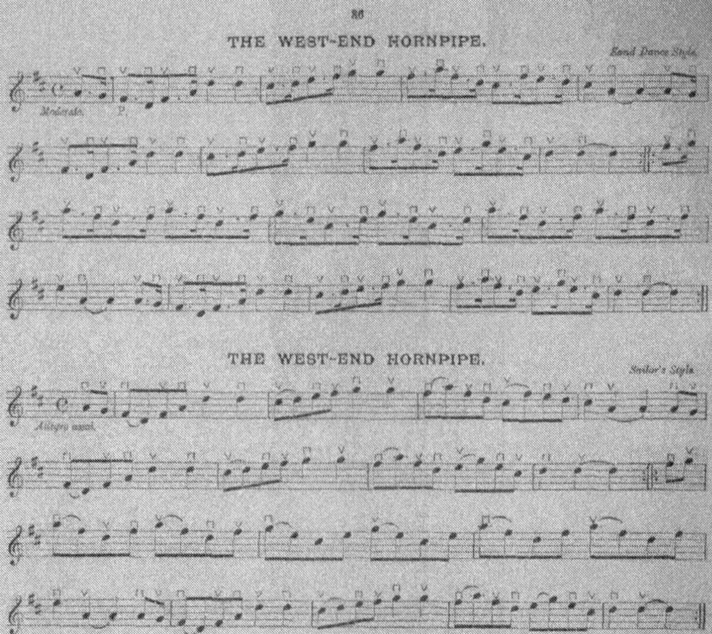

KEMP'S HORNPIPE.

An excellent study for the mastery of "The Sand Dance" style. The two leading notes at the beginning of each part must be accented very strongly with a down bow.

FISHER'S HORNPIPE.

In Newcastle Style and Stand Dance Style.

FISHER'S HORNPIPE.

Sailor's Style.

THE WONDER HORNPIPE.

Newcastle Style.

THE WONDER HORNPIPE.

THE WONDER HORNPIPE.

Sailor's Style.

THE CLIFF, OR RUBY HORNPIPE.

Moderato.

THE RIGHTS OF MAN HORNPIPE.

Newcastle Style.

THE RIGHTS OF MAN HORNPIPE.

Stage Dance Style.

THE RIGHTS OF MAN HORNPIPE.

Sailor's Style.

MILLICENT'S HORNPIPE.

Mixed Style.

Very little bow—not above an inch of the hair—must be used for the *staccato* triplets above, and the right spot is usually about 10 inches from the bottom of the hair, and 15 inches from the point.

MANCHESTER HORNPIPE.

Newcastle Style.

LIVERPOOL HORNPIPE.

BRISTOL HORNPIPE.

THE COLOSSEUM, OR KAY'S HORNPIPE.

THE NAVVIE ON THE LINE HORNPIPE.

MEG MERRILEES' HORNPIPE.

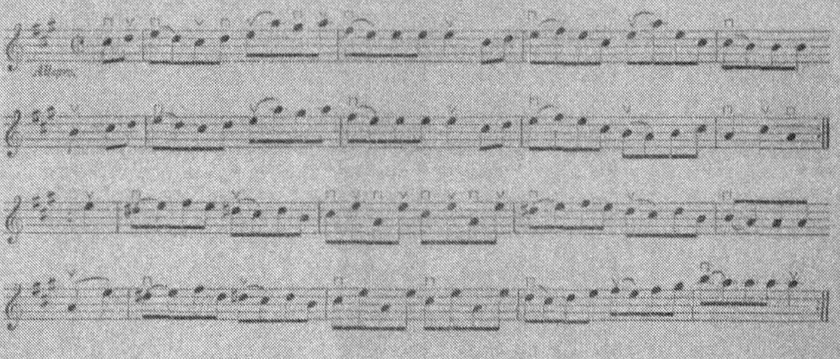

MARTON'S HORNPIPE.

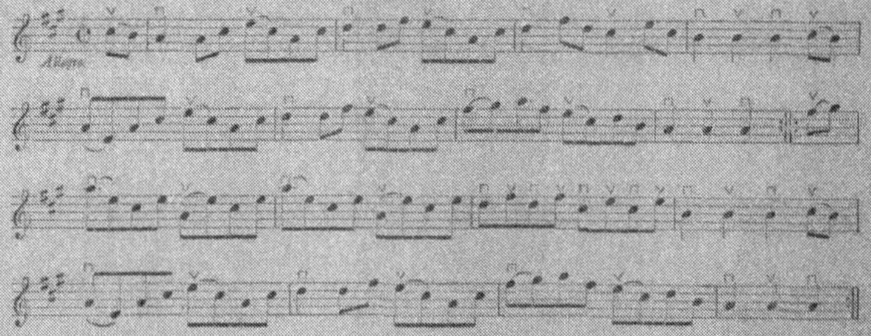

STATEN ISLAND, OR BURNS' HORNPIPE.

HARVEST HOME HORNPIPE.

KIRK'S HORNPIPE.

THE CHAMPION HORNPIPE.

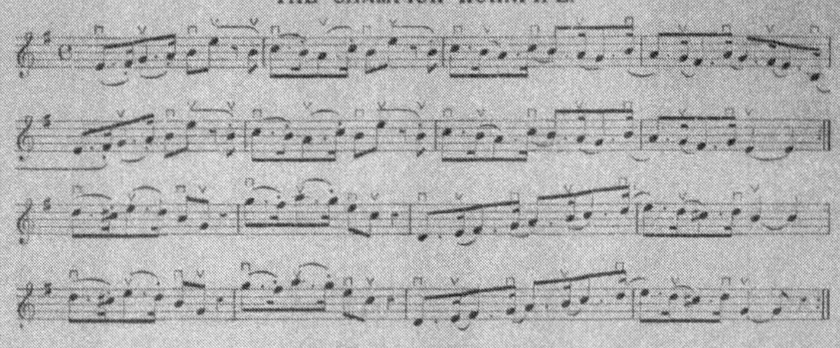

THE CHALLENGE BREAKDOWN.

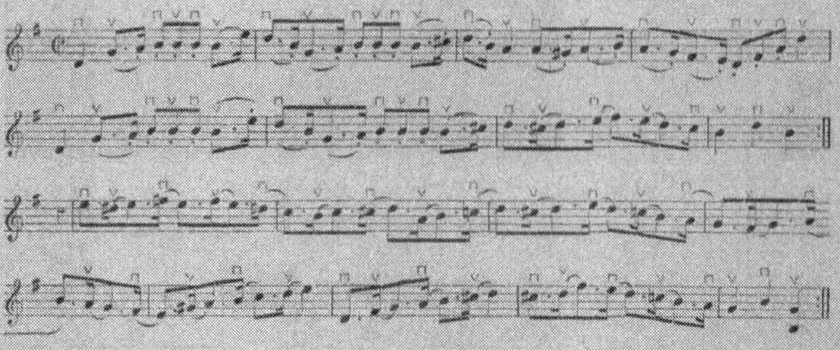

FAY'S HORNPIPE.

MARQUIS OF LORNE HORNPIPE.

JACK O' TAR HORNPIPE.

BLUE BONNETS HORNPIPE.

GLEN'S HORNPIPE.

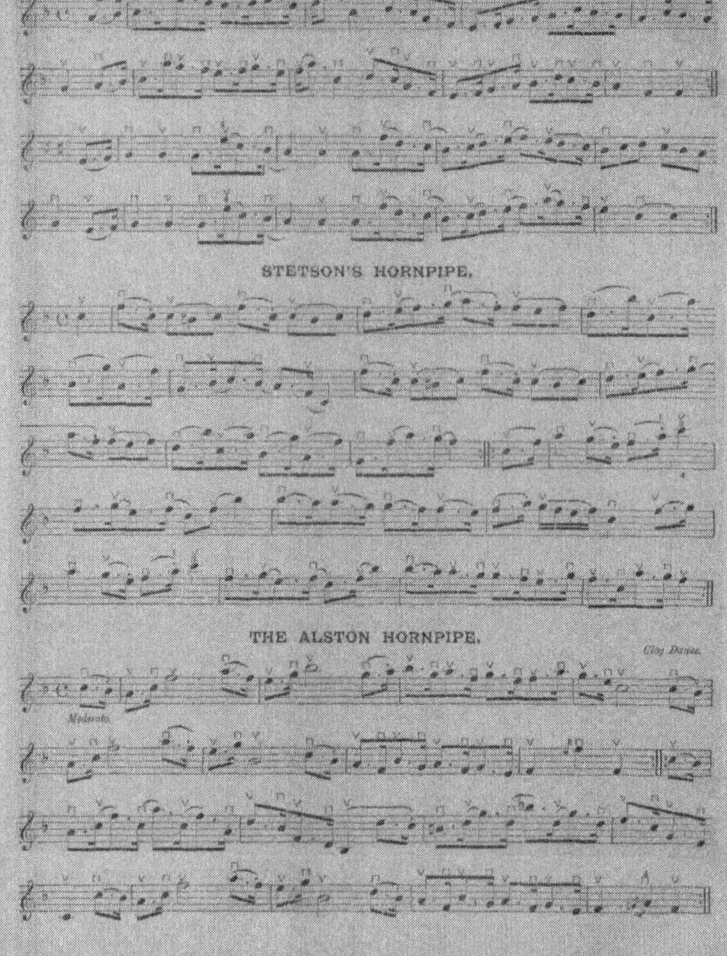

Friends of Wighton Shand Collection. Vol 15	Honeyman, William Crawford	Jimmy Shand Collection JS15, Honeyman's Collection [cover title]. *The Strathspey, Reel, and Hornpipe Tutor, being a concise analysis of the peculiar method of bowing these compositions, with numerous examples, and a selection of 92 favourite strathspeys and reels, and 50 favourite hornpipes* . (Edinburgh & London: E. Kohler & Son, 1898)

THE PEAR TREE HORNPIPE.

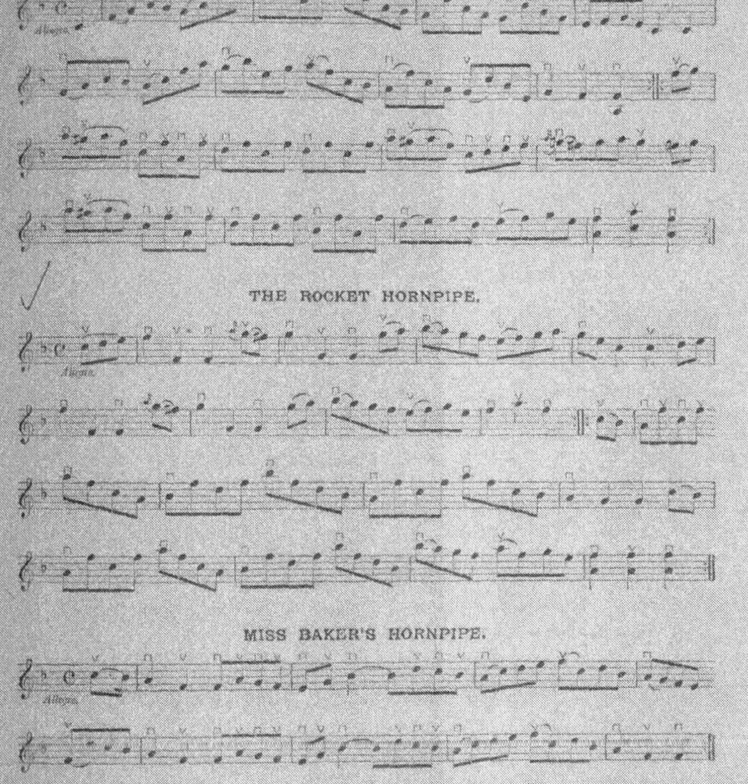

WASHINGTON, OR JENKINS' HORNPIPE.

THE COLLEGE HORNPIPE; OR, JACK'S THE LAD.

THE BROADSWORD HORNPIPE.

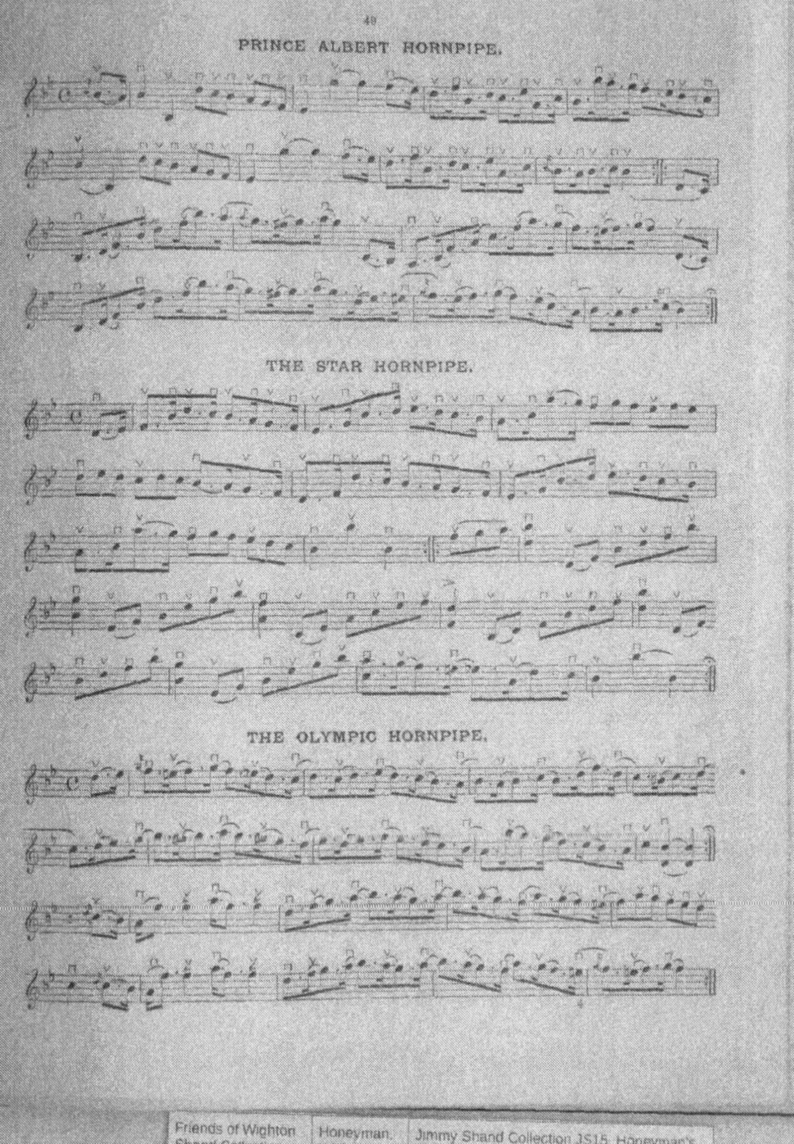
PRINCE ALBERT HORNPIPE.
THE STAR HORNPIPE.
THE OLYMPIC HORNPIPE.

THE THISTLE HORNPIPE.

THE FIREFLY HORNPIPE.

HIGH LEVEL BRIDGE HORNPIPE.

FACTORY SMOKE HORNPIPE.

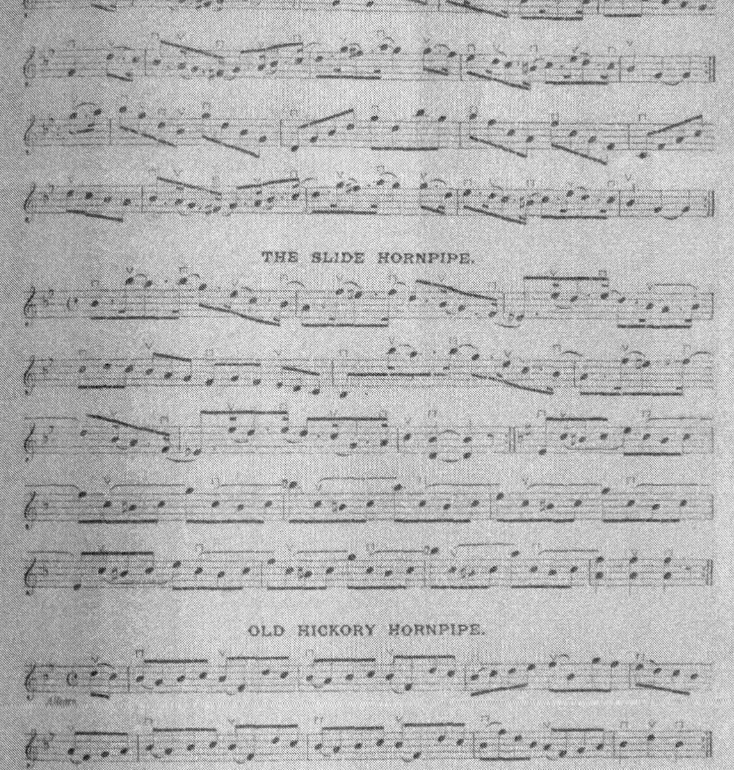

THE SLIDE HORNPIPE.

OLD HICKORY HORNPIPE.

BANK'S HORNPIPE, OR MRS. TAFF.

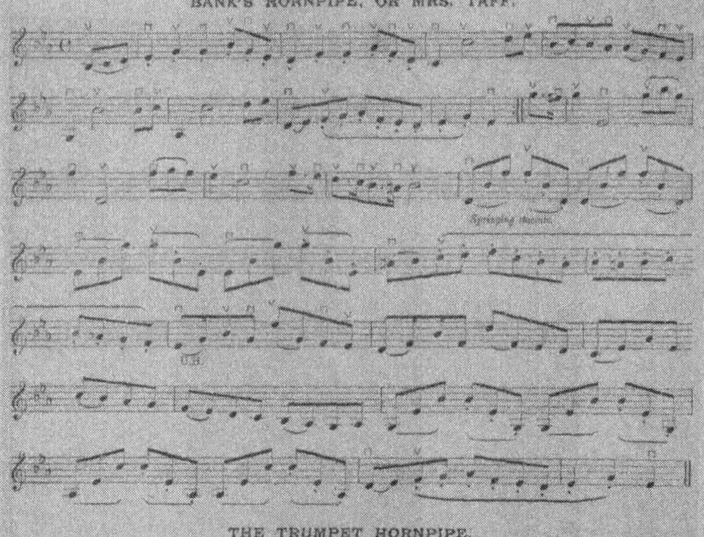

THE TRUMPET HORNPIPE.

www.ingramcontent.com/pod-product-compliance
Ingram Content Group UK Ltd.
Pitfield, Milton Keynes, MK11 3LW, UK
UKHW020628250226
10914UKWH00035B/278